Early detection of invasive species; surveillance, monitoring, and rapid response:

Eastern Rivers and Mountains Network summary report 2008–2009

Natural Resource Data Series NPS/ERMN/NRDS—2010/038

Jennifer Stingelin Keefer

The Pennsylvania State University
School of Forest Resources
309 Forest Resources Laboratory
University Park, Pennsylvania

March 2010

U.S. Department of the Interior
National Park Service
Natural Resource Program Center
Fort Collins, Colorado

The National Park Service, Natural Resource Program Center publishes a range of reports that address natural resource topics of interest and applicability to a broad audience in the National Park Service and others in natural resource management, including scientists, conservation and environmental constituencies, and the public.

The Natural Resource Data Series is intended for timely release of basic data sets and data summaries. Care has been taken to assure accuracy of raw data values, but a thorough analysis and interpretation of the data has not been completed. Consequently, the initial analyses of data in this report are provisional and subject to change.

All manuscripts in the series receive the appropriate level of peer review to ensure that the information is scientifically credible, technically accurate, appropriately written for the intended audience, and designed and published in a professional manner. Data in this report were collected and analyzed using methods based on established, peer-reviewed protocols and were analyzed and interpreted within the guidelines of the protocols.

Views, statements, findings, conclusions, recommendations, and data in this report are those of the author(s) and do not necessarily reflect views and policies of the National Park Service, U.S. Department of the Interior. Mention of trade names or commercial products does not constitute endorsement or recommendation for use by the National Park Service.

This report is available from (http://science.nature.nps.gov/im/units/ermn/) and the Natural Resource Publications Management website (http://www.nature.nps.gov/publications/NRPM).

Please cite this publication as:

Keefer, J. S. 2010. Early detection of invasive species; surveillance, monitoring, and rapid response: Eastern Rivers and Mountains Network summary report 2008–2009. Natural Resource Data Series NPS/ERMN/NRDS—2010/038. National Park Service, Fort Collins, Colorado.

NPS 962/101470, March 2010

Contents

Figures

Table

Executive Summary

Early detection monitoring of incipient invasive plants, animals and diseases was ranked among the top priorities in the Eastern Rivers and Mountains Network (ERMN) in the vital signs selection process due to the clear identification of, and concern about, the effects these organisms can have on park ecosystems. The known ecological impacts of invasive species include loss of threatened and endangered species, altered structure and composition of terrestrial and aquatic communities, and reduction in overall species diversity.

While long-term changes associated with invasive species are being monitored through other protocols, it is also critical to catch new populations of invasive species early in their invasion of new and sensitive habitats. Only when invasions are caught early will the chance of eradication remain high.

During invasive species early detection surveillance monitoring in 2008 and 2009, 20 new invasive plant and pest occurrences were documented at five parks in the ERMN by the vegetation monitoring crew, Delaware Water Gap National Recreation Area (DEWA) Biologist, Jeff Shreiner, New River Gorge National River (NERI) Biological Technician, Sophia DeMaio and the Animal and Plant Health Inspection Service (APHIS). New species occurrences included Japanese barberry (*Berberis thunbergii*), narrowleaf bittercress (*Cardamine impatiens*), privet (*Ligustrum* sp.), gypsy moth (*Lymantria dispar*), Amur corktree (*Phellodendron amurense*), Japanese knotweed (*Polygonum cuspidatum*), linden arrowwood (*Viburnum dilatatum*), emerald ash borer (*Agrilus planipennis*) and viburnum leaf beetle (*Pyrrhalta viburni*). Of the 15 new plant occurrences, 10 consisted of single specimens and/or small populations and were hand-pulled or chemically treated.

Introduction

During 2008, the Eastern Rivers and Mountains Network (ERMN) of the National Park Service (NPS) began early detection of invasive species surveillance monitoring throughout its nine parks. This monitoring effort is a component of the ERMN Vital Signs monitoring program (Marshall and Piekielek 2007), which is part of the nationwide NPS Inventory and Monitoring Program (Fancy et al. 2009).

One of the primary objectives of the ecological monitoring program in the ERMN is to detect incipient populations of invasive plants, animals and diseases before they have a chance to become widely established. To achieve this objective, target "watch" species lists were developed; target species identification information was maintained and distributed to all ERMN field crews and other interested cooperators, resource managers, and volunteers; and an early detection reporting and tracking system that disseminates information on potential infestations in a timely and efficient manner was developed. The primary goal of this protocol is to assist park managers to identify high priority invasive species, quickly disseminate new occurrence information to all interested parties (NPS, public, private, etc.), assess the risk presented by incipient populations, and assist with management of newly detected species.

An "invasive species" is an alien species whose introduction does or is likely to cause economic or environmental harm or harm to human health (USPEO 1999). Early detection followed by rapid response can detect and eradicate incipient populations of invasive species before they have a chance to become widely established, thus eliminating the need for costly and resource intensive control programs (Ashton and Mitchell 1989; OTA 1993; Atkinson 1997; Myers et al. 2000; Timmins and Braithwaite 2001; Harris et al. 2001; Rejmanek and Pitcairn 2002). Only when invasions are caught early will the chance of eradication remain high (Rozenfelds et al. 1999; NISC 2008). Eradication of established invasive species is difficult, if not impossible in many cases, but early detection and associated management responses have proven effective in reducing, if not eliminating, the associated costs and consequences (MacDonald et al. 1989; Braithwaite 2000).

At the time this report was prepared, the Early Detection of Invasive Species Surveillance Monitoring and Rapid Response Protocol (Keefer et al. 2010) had been developed, written, and received internal peer review, but had not undergone the final peer review process. This report was intended to provide preliminary results to the natural resource managers at Allegheny Portage Railroad National Historic Site (ALPO), Bluestone National Scenic River (BLUE), Delaware Water Gap National Recreation Area (DEWA), Fort Necessity National Battlefield (FONE), Friendship Hill National Historic Site (FRHI), Gauley River National Recreation Area (GARI), Johnstown Flood National Memorial (JOFL), New River Gorge National River (NERI), and Upper Delaware Scenic and Recreational River (UPDE).

Methods

Although a brief overview of the invasive species early detection (ISED) methods is provided here, a detailed explanation of the background, rationale, and methods, in addition to Standard Operating Procedures are provided in the protocol (Keefer et al. 2010).

Selecting Early Detection Species
The process for selecting a short list of invasive species for inclusion in the ISED program for each park in the ERMN consisted of four main components: 1) review existing park datasets and literature and compile a list of all invasive plant and pest species known or thought to occur in the parks; 2) eliminate all common and well-established species as candidates for "early detection;" 3) consult relevant existing invasive species data sources from nearby parks, towns, counties, and states for incipient invasive species not yet present in the parks and add them to the candidate ISED list; and 4) conduct more extensive research on each candidate species and consult with park natural resource managers to narrow down and finalize each park ISED list (Keefer et al. 2010). At the conclusion of this process each park's final ISED list (Table 1) generally consists of between 10 and 20 species.

Opportunistic Sampling
"Every person working or recreating in a national park has the potential to serve as an early detector" (Williams et al. 2007). Knowledgeable crew members provided an additional "set of eyes and ears" to detect invasive species occurrences while they were collecting data at monitoring sites, walking to and from monitoring sites, and driving along park roads. Invasive plants and pests present on each park's ISED list (Table 1) were sought during routine vegetation monitoring (Perles et al. 2009). Park natural resource managers, Exotic Plant Management Teams (EPMT), volunteers, and other NPS individuals with scientific backgrounds also served as early detectors during their daily park activities.

Invasive Species Early Detection Field Guide
To assist with the identification of early detection species and designate specific lists of early detection species per park, ISED guides were provided to monitoring crews and interested parties. Hand-held, weather proof pocket guides provided cost-free by the USDA Forest Service, "Invasive Plants Field and Reference Guide: An Ecological Perspective of Plant Invaders of Forests and Woodlands (USFS field guide)," http://www.treesearch.fs.fed.us/pubs/20715, in addition to a supplemental identification field guide developed by the ERMN, were used to distribute target species identification information. Production of the "Early Detection of Invasive Species Surveillance Monitoring Field Guide" and nine species cards was completed in summer 2009. Each completed species card, as well as the entire field guide, were posted on the ERMN web site and are available for download at http://science.nature.nps.gov/im/units/ermn/monitoring/earlydetection.cfm.

Alert System
Data acquired from ISED is time sensitive and all new detections are immediately reported through the appropriate chain of command. Each observer or monitoring crew leader is responsible for alerting the designated park contact (DPC) and Invasive Species Early Detection Coordinator (ISEDC) to all new species detections. In cases where noxious weeds or high

Table 1. List of plant and pest species included in the Invasive Species Early Detection (ISED) program for the Eastern Rivers and Mountains Network (ERMN) by park and taxa category. Parks include: Allegheny Portage Railroad National Historic Site (ALPO), Bluestone National Scenic River (BLUE), Delaware Water Gap National Recreation Area (DEWA), Fort Necessity National Battlefield (FONE), Friendship Hill National Historic Site (FRHI), Gauley River National Recreation Area (GARI), Johnstown Flood National Memorial (JOFL), New River Gorge National River (NERI), and Upper Delaware Scenic and Recreational River (UPDE). ED = Early detection species. P/ED = Present within the park in small numbers, but early detection is still warranted to prevent the spread to other areas of the park

Scientific Name	Common Name	Taxa Category	ALPO	BLUE	DEWA	FONE	FRHI	GARI	JOFL	NERI	UPDE
Acer platanoides	Norway maple	PLANT		ED				ED	ED	ED	
Adelges tsugae	hemlock wooly adelgid	PEST	P/ED			ED	ED				ED
Agrilus planipennis	emerald ash borer	PEST	ED	ED	ED	ED	ED	ED	ED		ED
Ailanthus altissima	tree of heaven	PLANT		ED	ED	ED		ED	ED		ED
Alliaria petiolata	garlic mustard	PLANT					ED				
Anoplophora glabripennis	Asian long-horned beetle	PEST	ED		ED	ED	ED		ED		ED
Aralia elata	Japanese aralia	PLANT			ED						ED
Berberis thunbergii	Japanese barberry	PLANT		ED						P/ED	
Cardamine impatiens	narrowleaf bittercress	PLANT	ED		P/ED	ED	ED				ED
Celastrus orbiculatus	oriental bittersweet	PLANT		ED				ED	ED		
Cynanchum louiseae/C. rossicum	Louise's & European swallow-worts	PLANT			ED						ED
Dioscorea oppositifolia	Chinese yam	PLANT		P/ED							
Euonymus alatus	winged burning bush	PLANT				ED	ED	ED			
Frangula alnus	glossy buckthorn	PLANT	ED	ED	ED	ED	ED	ED	ED	ED	
Heracleum mantegazzium	giant hogweed	PLANT	ED	ED	ED	ED	ED	ED	ED	ED	ED
Lespedeza cuneata	Chinese lespedeza	PLANT						P/ED			
Ligustrum obtusifolium/L. vulgare	border/European privets	PLANT			P/ED		P/ED				ED
Lonicera japonica	Japanese honeysuckle	PLANT							ED		ED
Lythrum salicaria	purple loosestrife	PLANT						ED			
Microstegium vimineum	Japanese stiltgrass	PLANT							ED		
Oplismenus hirtellus ssp. undulatifolius	wavyleaf basketgrass	PLANT	ED	ED	ED	ED	ED	ED	ED		ED
Phragmites australis	phragmites	PLANT		ED	P/ED	P/ED	ED	ED			
Polygonum cuspidatum/sachalinense	Japanese/giant knotweed	PLANT		P/ED				P/ED			
Polygonum perfoliatum	mile-a-minute	PLANT	P/ED	ED	P/ED	ED	ED	ED	ED	ED	ED
Pueraria montana var. lobata	kudzu	PLANT	ED	ED	ED	ED	ED	ED	ED	ED	ED
Pyrrhalta viburni	viburnum leaf beetle	PEST	ED	ED	ED	ED	ED	ED	ED		ED
Ranunculus ficaria	lesser celandine	PLANT		ED	ED	ED	ED	ED		ED	ED
Rhamnus cathartica	common buckthorn	PLANT			ED	ED	ED	ED	ED	P/ED	ED
Sirex noctilio	Sirex woodwasp	PEST	ED	ED	ED	ED	ED	ED	ED	ED	ED

4

priority pests are detected, the ISEDC will follow-up with each DPC and may assist with alerting relevant outside agencies.

Rapid Response
Rapid responses to invasions are effective and can prevent the spread and permanent establishment of invasive species. Coordinating and/or executing a rapid response is primarily the responsibility of the respective park resource manager(s) in which the infestation was detected. Rapid response should include positive species identification and management/eradication activities, and may involve coordination with the EPMT, agencies such as the Bureau of Plant Industry and the Animal and Plant Health Inspection Service (APHIS) within the U.S. Department of Agriculture, local weed management organizations, Network and park personnel, as well as park interns. Each response was based on the individual needs of the park and the resources available (Figure 1) (Keefer et al. 2010).

Data Management and Reporting
Currently, the ERMN is using a Microsoft Excel spreadsheet to keep track of all new invasive species occurrences; however, we are in the process of developing the ISED database, which is a Microsoft Access based and Natural Resource Database Template (NRDT) compliant relational database. This database will keep track of new species occurrences (documents presence), assessments, and all management or rapid responses at the documented location.

The Early Detection and Distribution Mapping System (EDDMapS), in conjunction with the ERMN Web site, will provide a data entry port, alert system, and a one-stop resource for invasive species information, including links to other invasive species Web sites, photos, important contacts, and other pertinent information. To view the current ERMN web site, visit: http://science.nature.nps.gov/im/units/ermn/monitoring/EarlyDetection.cfm.

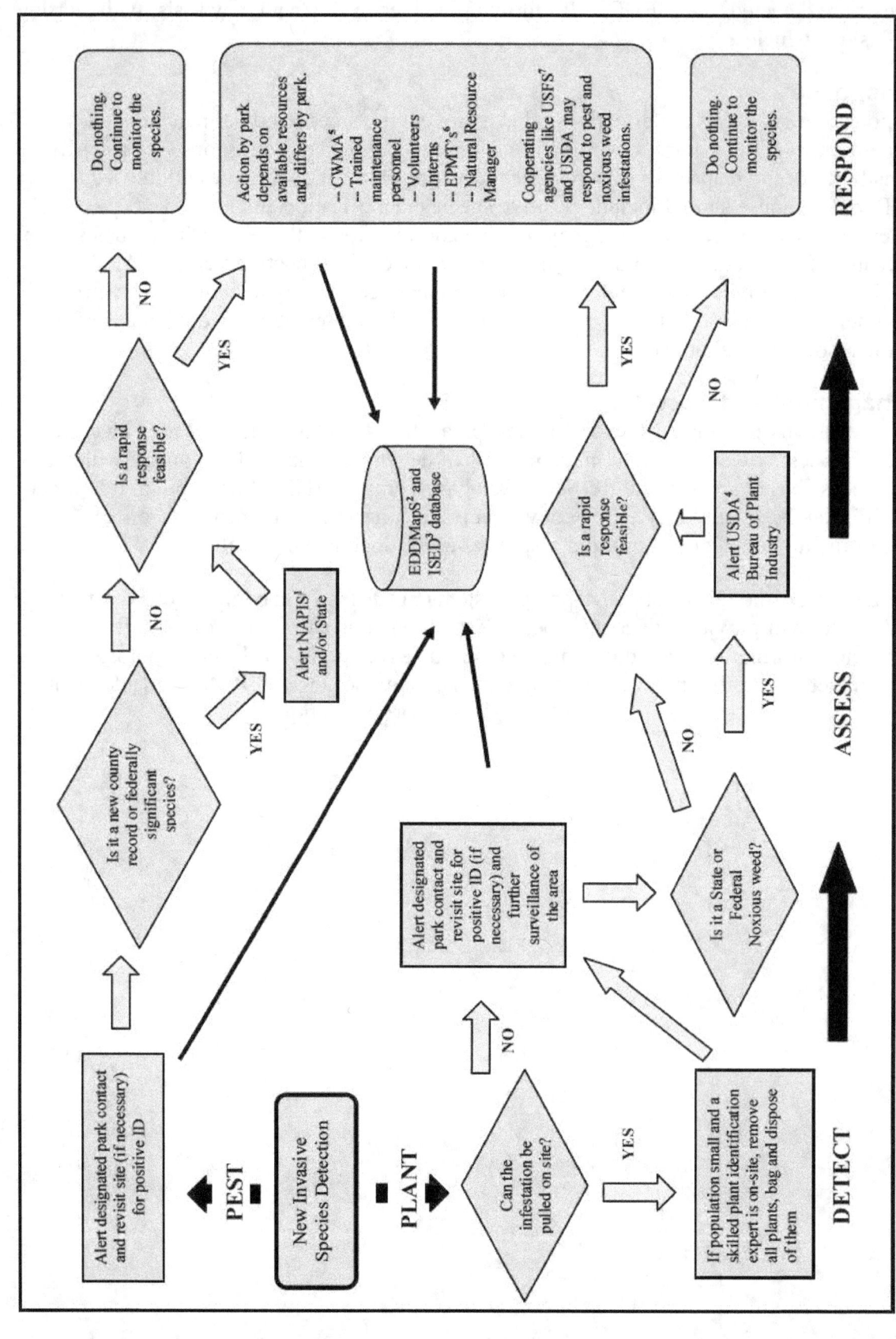

Figure 1. Early Detection of Invasive Species Rapid Response system for the Eastern Rivers and Mountains Network (ERMN).

1. National Agricultural Pest Information System (NAPIS); 2. Early Detection & Distribution Mapping System (EDDMapS); 3. Invasive Species Early Detection (ISED); 4. United States Department of Agriculture (USDA); 5. Cooperative Weed Management Area (CWMA); 6. Exotic Plant Management Team (EPMT); 7. United States Forest Service (USFS).

Results and Discussion

National Park Service Units Studies
Allegheny Portage Railroad National Historic Site (ALPO)
No new invasive species early detections were recorded at ALPO by the vegetation monitoring crew or park personnel in 2008 or 2009. The ALPO invasive species early detection list will be re-evaluated and updated as necessary during winter 2009.

Bluestone National Scenic River (BLUE)
No new invasive species early detections were recorded at BLUE by the vegetation monitoring crew or park personnel in 2008 or 2009; however, one previous observation of Japanese knotweed (*Polygonum cuspidatum*) discovered by botanist Jim Vanderhorst on November 28, 2003, was re-visited and treated as a result of the development and initiation of the ISED protocol (Figure 2). Japanese knotweed was observed in one location near the Little Bluestone River and upstream of the Bluestone Lodge. A combination treatment of 5 percent glyphosate (Accord®) and 0.5 percent Isopropylamine salt of Imazapyr (Habitat®) was applied as a foliar spray. The rapid response crew consisted of Sophia DeMaio and Don DeFilipps, both biological technicians at NERI (Sophia DeMaio, personal communication, December 15, 2009).

The BLUE invasive species early detection list will be re-evaluated and updated as necessary during winter 2009. Based on APHIS monitoring traps, BLUE is still free of emerald ash borer (John Perez, personal communication, October 9, 2009).

See Appendix to view a summary score card of early detection plant and pest species for BLUE.

Delaware Water Gap National Recreation Area (DEWA)
Four new early detection species, narrowleaf bittercress (*Cardamine impatiens*), viburnum leaf beetle (*Pyrrhalta viburni*), linden arrowwood (*Viburnum dilatatum*) and Amur corktree (*Phellodendron amurense*), were detected at DEWA in 2008 and 2009 (Figures 3 and 4). Linden arrowwood and Amur corktree were not on the 2008/2009 early detection list, but were slated to be added to the 2010 early detection list.

Narrowleaf bittercress was observed in three new locations by the ERMN vegetation monitoring crew: 1) in floodplain off of Peters Canoe Camp Road, Sussex Co., NJ; (2) in a plantation between Route 209 and river, Pike Co., PA; and (3) on the river side of Old Mine Road north of mile marker 22, Sussex Co., NJ. Plants in the first infestation were pulled, bagged, and disposed of. After a few hours searching the floodplain where the plants were discovered, Park Biologist, Jeff Shreiner, did not discover any new plants. Plants in the second infestation were also hand-pulled, bagged, and removed from the site; however, it is uncertain whether there are additional plants in the vicinity of the original infestation. There are currently plans to search for and treat any remaining plants in the vicinity of the second infestation and treat the larger population off of Old Mine Road in 2010 (Jeff Shreiner, personnel communication, December 22, 2009).

Viburnum leaf beetle evidence was observed at three locations in Sussex County, New Jersey, by the ERMN vegetation monitoring crew: 1) floodplain swamp along Flatbrook, just west of Mountain Trail Rd; (2) off of horse path at end of Van Ness Road; and 3) swampy floodplain near pull-off off of Route 615. Host species were southern arrowwood (*Viburnum dentatum*) and

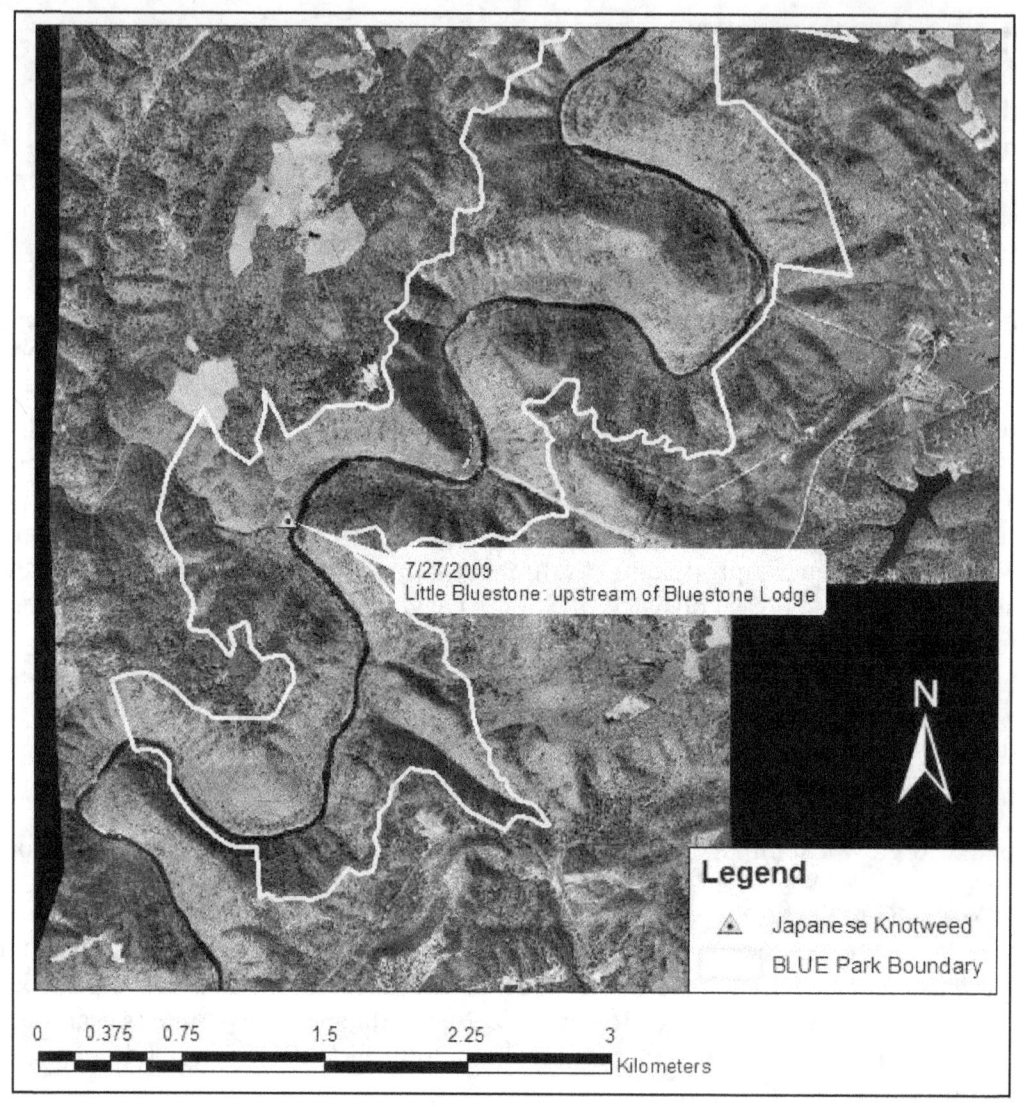

7/27/2009
Little Bluestone: upstream of Bluestone Lodge

Legend

⚠ Japanese Knotweed

BLUE Park Boundary

| 0 | 0.375 | 0.75 | 1.5 | 2.25 | 3 |
Kilometers

Figure 2. Japanese knotweed (*Polygonum cuspidatum*) early detection location in Bluestone National Scenic River (BLUE).

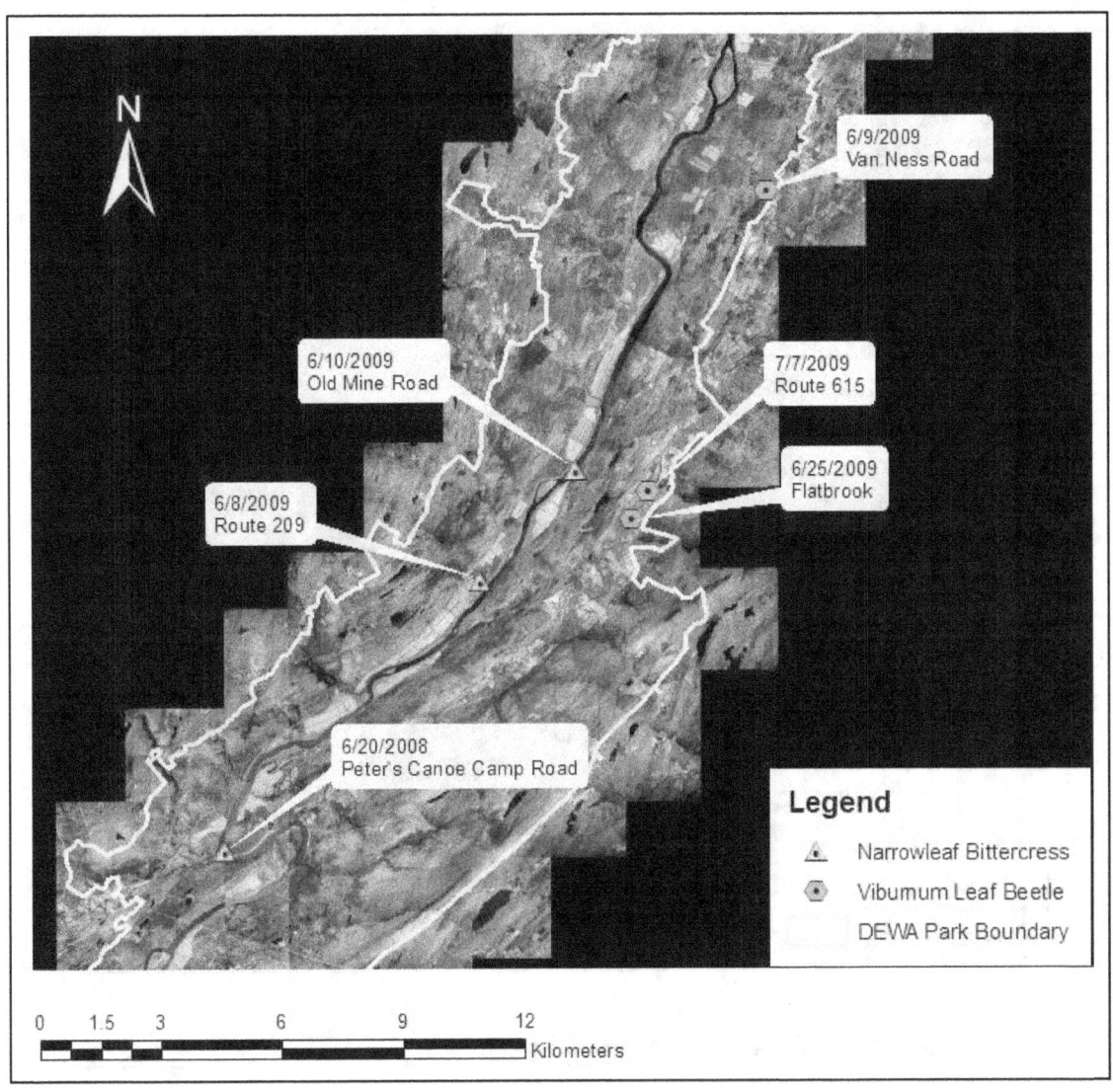

Figure 3. Narrowleaf bittercress (*Cardamine impatiens*) and viburnum leaf beetle (*Pyrrhalta viburni*) early detection locations in Delaware Water Gap National Recreation Area (DEWA).

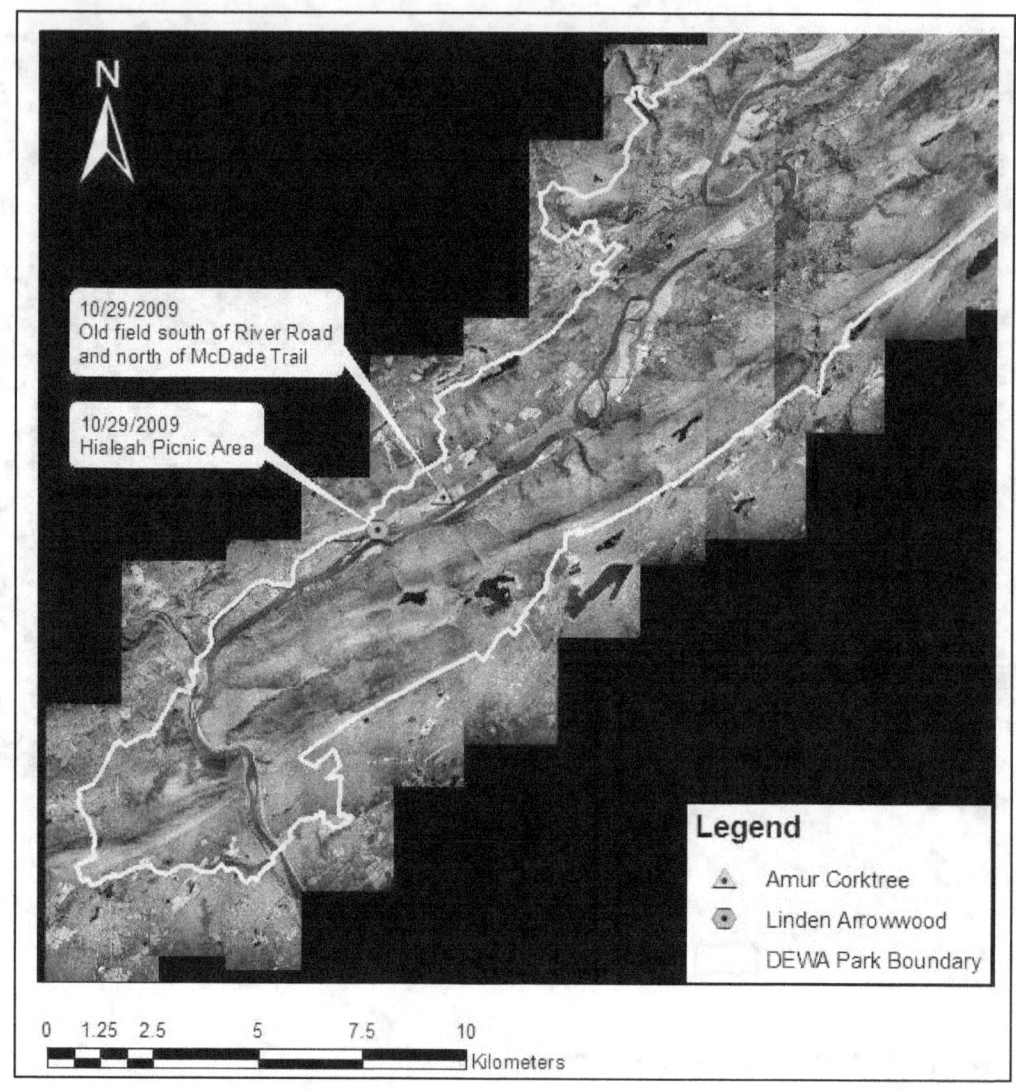

Figure 4. Amur corktree (*Phellodendron amurense*) and linden arrowwood (*Viburnum dilatatum*) early detection locations in Delaware Water Gap National Recreation Area (DEWA).

northern arrowwood (*Viburnum recognitum*) and exhibited branch death, defoliation, and foliar injury. Although no adult beetles or larvae were observed, the damage was highly suspicious.

Evidence was reported to the Department of Agriculture on January 7, 2010, but confirmation of the identity must occur before any report can be registered in the National Agricultural Pest Information System (NAPIS). Efforts to observe and positively identify the organism will continue in 2010 (Jeff Shreiner, personal communication, October 6, 2009).

Linden arrowwood was observed at one location in Monroe County, Pennsylvania, by Jeff Shreiner, park Biologist: Hialeah Picnic area; along main drive paralleling the Delaware River, just southwest of restroom on north side of drive. One shrub with two stems was observed. All fruits were removed from the site and a basal bark treatment consisting of 25% triclopyr (Garlon® 4) was employed to treat both stems.

Amur corktree was observed at one location in Monroe County, Pennsylvania, by Jeff Shreiner, park Biologist: old field south of River Road and north of McDade Trail, about 1 km (0.6 mi) southwest of Smithfield Beach. A total of nine trees were observed in three separate locations, about 140 m (459 ft) apart from one another. One tree was located on a road bank on River Road opposite a pull-off; six trees (two with berries) were located in an old field on the south side of River Road; and two were located near McDade Trail along a service road just north of the trail. Basal bark treatments consisting of 25% triclopyr (Garlon® 4) were employed to treat all nine stems the same day as discovery.

See Appendix to view a summary score card of early detection plant and pest species for DEWA.

Fort Necessity National Battlefield (FONE)
No new invasive species early detections were recorded at FONE by the vegetation monitoring crew or park personnel in 2008 or 2009. The FONE invasive species early detection list will be re-evaluated and updated as necessary during winter 2009.

Friendship Hill National Historic Site (FRHI)
One new early detection species, privet (*Ligustrum* sp.), was detected at FRHI in 2008 (Figure 5). Privet was observed in a field to the west of New Geneva Road (PA 166), just off Pekar Road, by the ERMN vegetation monitoring crew. The main colony is well established and covers approximately a 50–100 m^2 (538–1,076 ft^2) area. There are currently no treatment plans.

See Appendix to view a summary score card of early detection plant and pest species for FRHI.

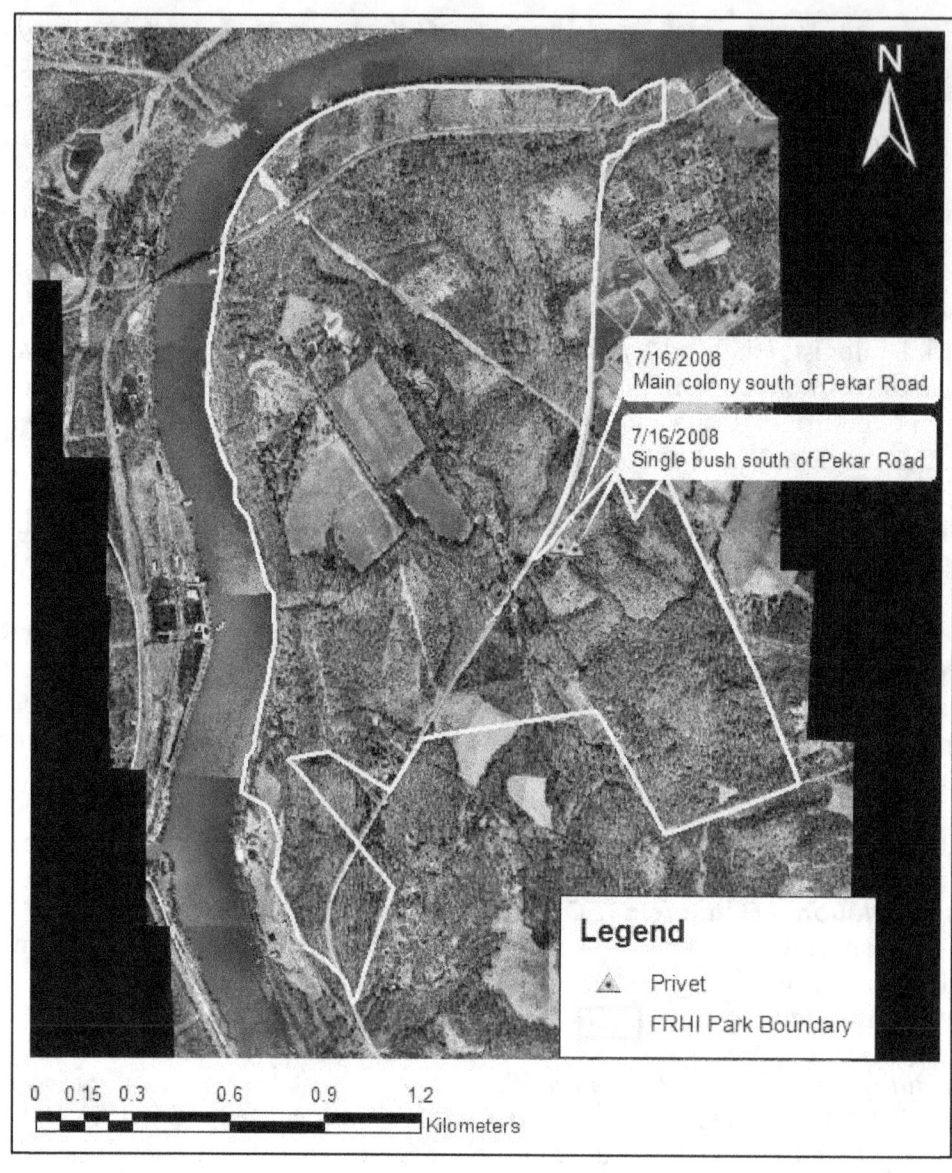

Figure 5. Privet (*Ligustrum* spp.) early detection locations in Friendship Hill National Historic Site (FRHI).

Gauley River National Recreation Area (GARI)

One new early detection species, Japanese knotweed (*Polygonum cuspidatum*), was detected at GARI in 2008 and 2009 (Figure 6). Japanese knotweed was observed in two new locations by the ERMN vegetation monitoring crew: (1) Bottom of the Woods Ferry Road access on both sides of the newly improved road near the railroad grade in Fayette County, WV; and (2) Confluence of Peter's Creek and the Gauley River in the floodplain of the northern shore, Raleigh Co., WV. Initially there were no plans to target these populations at GARI due to access issues with privately owned land, scarce resources (no permanent staff), lack of funding, and logistical hurdles (John Perez, personal communication, October 9, 2009). However, plans to target these populations are now being explored (John Perez, personal communication, December 15, 2009). Based on APHIS monitoring traps, GARI is still free of emerald ash borer (John Perez, personal communication, October 9, 2009).

See Appendix to view a summary score card of early detection plant and pest species for GARI.

Johnstown Flood National Memorial (JOFL)

No new invasive species early detections were recorded at JOFL by the vegetation monitoring crew or park personnel in 2008 or 2009. The JOFL invasive species early detection list will be re-evaluated and updated as necessary during winter 2009.

New River Gorge National River (NERI)

Three new early detection species, Japanese barberry (*Berberis thunbergii*), emerald ash borer (*Agrilus planipennis*), and gypsy moth (*Lymantria dispar*), were detected at NERI in 2009 (Figures 7 and 8). Japanese barberry was observed in three new locations by the ERMN vegetation monitoring crew and three locations by park personnel: 1) Landscaping in the front yard of the NPS-owned house in Prince, Fayette County; 2) Near the switchback on the road down to the Grandview sandbar, Raleigh County; 3) Off of McKendree Road, Fayette County; 4) Sandstone Falls, Raleigh County; 5) Red Ash Island, Fayette County; and (6) near Thurmond, Fayette County. The single specimen located in the landscaping at the NPS-owned property was pulled, bagged, and disposed of by the vegetation monitoring crew. Basal bark treatments consisting of 44.3 percent triclopyr (Garlon® 4) were employed to treat all of the additional barberry plants at Sandstone Falls and on Red Ash Island and a combination treatment of 5 percent glyphosate (Accord®) and 0.5 percent Isopropylamine salt of Imazapyr (Habitat®) was applied as a foliar spray at the Thurmond site. The rapid response crew consisted of Sophia DeMaio and Don DeFilipps, both biological technicians at NERI (Sophia DeMaio, personal communication, September 21, 2009 and October 1, 2009).

In July 2009, Animal and Plant Health Inspection Service (APHIS) confirmed the presence of emerald ash borer in one of their purple traps inside the boundary of NERI (John Perez, personal communication, 7/21/2009). Since the July detection, emerald ash borer were trapped in four additional locations (1 per trap) (Sophia DeMaio, personal communication, 12/15/2009). The trap location of the initial detection is approximately 4.8 km (3 mi) south of the known infestation on the ACE property in Minden, Fayette County, WV. In addition to the trap detections, some ash tree decline, especially in the tree tops, was also detected. John Perez, Biologist at NERI, is currently working with APHIS, the National Park Service, and other outside agencies to develop a response protocol.

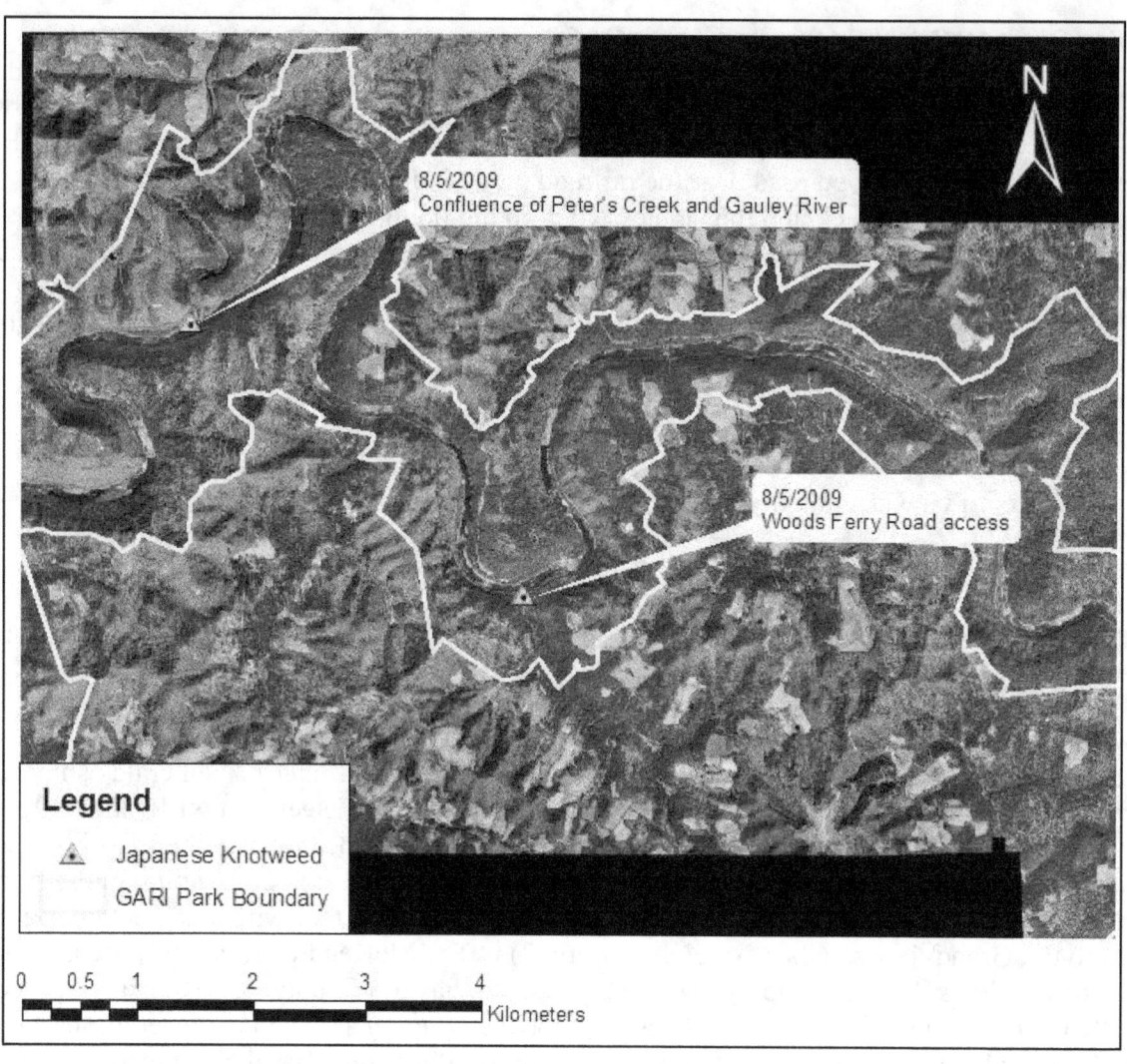

Figure 6. Japanese knotweed (*Polygonum cuspidatum*) early detection locations in Gauley River National Recreation Area (GARI).

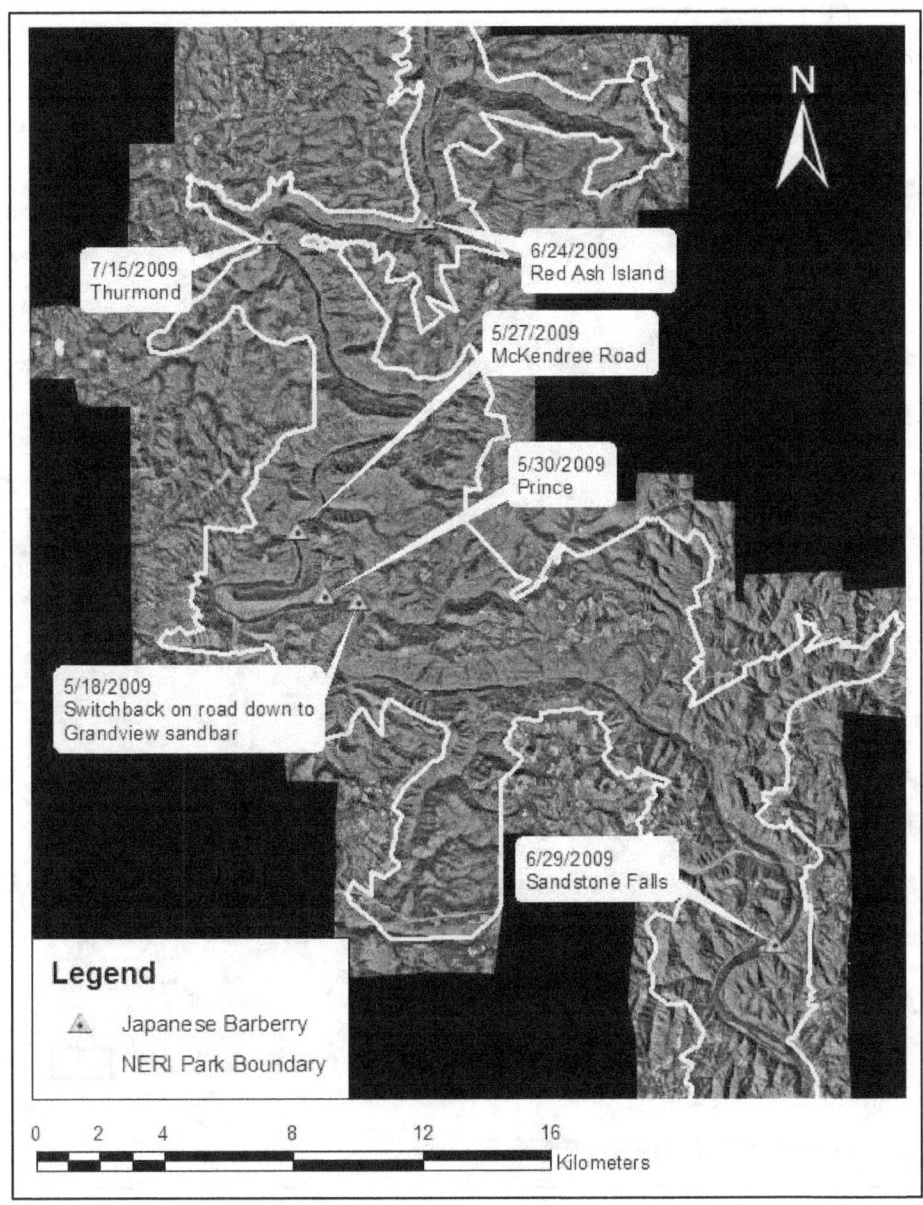

Figure 7. Japanese barberry (*Berberis thunbergii*) early detection locations in New River Gorge National River (NERI).

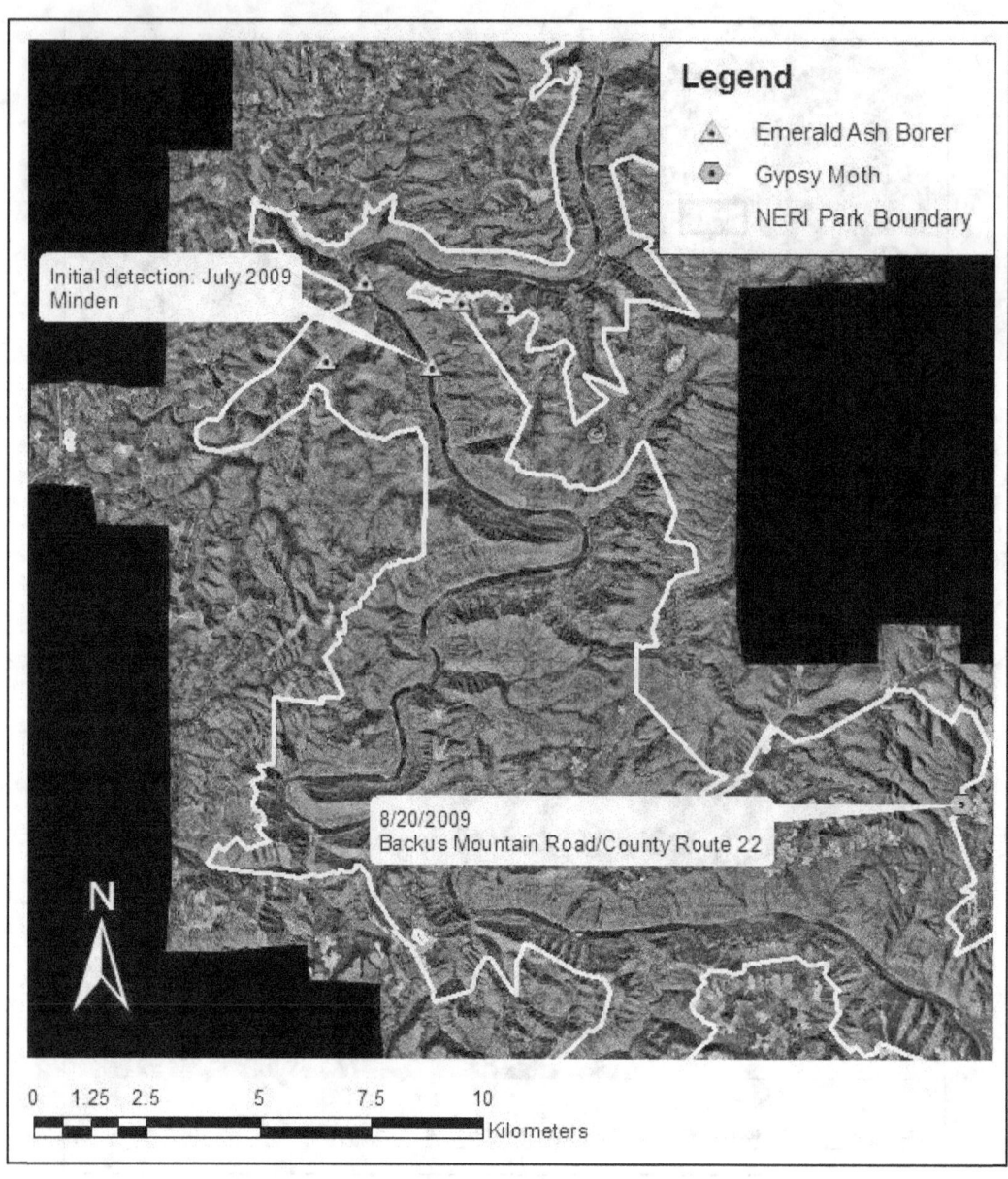

Legend
- ⬚ Emerald Ash Borer
- ⬡ Gypsy Moth
- ▭ NERI Park Boundary

Initial detection: July 2009
Minden

8/20/2009
Backus Mountain Road/County Route 22

N

0   1.25   2.5   5   7.5   10
Kilometers

Figure 8. Emerald ash borer (*Agrilus planipennis)* and gypsy moth (*Lymantria dispar*) early detection locations in New River Gorge National River (NERI).

In October 2009 the US Forest Service began gathering information on the infestation of emerald ash borer that will be used in the preparation of a Biological Assessment. The park is seeking Forest Pest funding for fiscal year 2010 to begin treatments on select ash trees (John Perez, personal communication, October 9, 2009).

A gypsy moth egg mass was also discovered for the first time in NERI by the vegetation monitoring crew (Figure 9). The egg mass and one dried pupa were discovered on the bole of a red maple within a permanent vegetation monitoring plot (NERI.182) in Fayette County. This new life stage occurrence and confirmation of a breeding population was reported to the U.S. Department of Agriculture (John Perez, personal communication, December 11, 2009).

See Appendix to view a summary score card of early detection plant and pest species for NERI.

Upper Delaware National Scenic and Recreational River (UPDE)
No new invasive species early detections were recorded at UPDE by park personnel in 2008 or 2009. The UPDE invasive species early detection list will be re-evaluated and updated as necessary during winter 2009.

Invasive Species Occurrence Mapping
All new invasive plant species occurrences were mapped and are available for viewing in the Early Detection and Distribution Mapping System (EDDMapS). To view these data in EDDMapS, visit: http://www.eddmaps.org/ and click on "Distribution Maps." Choose a species, and then click on a state and then a county to see information about the species.

Figure 9. Gypsy moth (*Lymantria dispar*) egg mass on red maple (*Acer rubrum*) at New River Gorge National River (NERI). Photo taken by Stephanie Perles.

Looking Ahead to 2010

New for the Spring 2010 field seasons will be the addition of several species of aquatic invasive vegetation and diatoms to the ISED program. For example, Didymo (*Didymosphenia geminata*), is a diatom that can smother entire stream beds with mats up to 20 cm (7.8 in) thick (Spaulding and Elwell 2007). Other aquatic plants include, but are not limited to, water chestnut (*Trapa natans*) and hydrilla (*Hydrilla verticillata*) that form dense mats that often shade out native vegetation and interfere with boaters and swimmers in recreational waters (Milon et al. 1986; Naylor 2003). Each aquatic species will be reviewed for possible inclusion into each park list.

In addition to the new aquatic species, during Winter 2009/2010 each park ISED list will be reviewed by Network staff, park natural resource managers, and other pertinent contacts to ensure that the list is current and contains the top priority species (See Updating Invasive Species Early Detection Lists SOP 1; Keefer et al. 2010). New invasive species threats will be evaluated for possible inclusion in a park's ISED list, while the prior year's list of species should be evaluated to determine if any should be removed from the list.

Literature Cited

Ashton, P. J., and D. S. Mitchell. 1989. Aquatic Plants: Patterns and Modes of Invasion, Attributes of Invading Species and Assessment of Control Programmes. Pgs. 111–154 *In* Biological Invasions: A Global Perspective. J. A. Drake, H. A. Mooney, F. di Castri, R. H. Groves, F. J. Kruger, M. Rejmanek, and M. Williamson (Eds.). John Wiley & Sons, Ltd. Chichester, England.

Atkinson, I. A. E. 1997. Problem weeds on New Zealand islands. Science Conservation 45. Wellington, Department of Conservation.

Braithwaite, H. 2000. Weed Surveillance Plan for the Department of Conservation. Wellington, Department of Conservation.

Fancy, S. G., J. E. Gross, and S. L. Carter. 2009. Monitoring the condition of natural resources in US national parks. Environmental Monitoring Assessment. 151:161–174.

Harris, S., J. Brown, and S. Timmins. 2001. Weed Surveillance — How Often to Search? Science for Conservation 175.

Keefer, J. S., M. R. Marshall, and B. R. Mitchell. 2010. Early Detection of Invasive Species— Surveillance and Rapid Response for the Eastern Rivers and Mountains and Northeast Temperate Networks. Natural Resource Report NPS/ERMN/NRR–2009/00X. National Park Service, Fort Collins, CO.

MacDonald, I. A.W., L. L. Loope, M. B. Usher, O. Harmann. 1989. Wildlife conservation and the invasion of nature reserves by exotic species: a global perspective. *In* Biological Invasions: a global perspective. Wiley and Sons. Drake, J., F. diCastri, R. Groves, F. Kruger, H. A. Mooney, M. Rejmanek, and M. Williamson, (eds.). Chichester, England.

Marshall, M. R., and N. B. Piekielek. 2007. Eastern Rivers and Mountains Network Ecological Monitoring Plan. Natural Resource Report NPS/ERMN/NRR—2007/017. National Park Service. Fort Collins, CO.

Milon, J. W., J. Yingling and J. E. Reynolds. 1986. An economic analysis of the benefits of aquatic weed control in North-Central Florida, Economics Report No. 113, Food and Resource Economics, Agricultural Experiment Station, Institute of Food and Agricultural Sciences, University of Florida, Gainesville 32611.

Myers, J. H., D. Simberloff, A. M. Kuris, and J. R. Carey. 2000. Eradication Revisited: Dealing with Exotic Species. Trends in Ecology and Evolution 15(8):316–320.

National Invasive Species Council (NISC). 2008. 2008-2012 National Invasive Species Management Plan.

Naylor, Mike. 2003. Water Chestnut (Trapa natans) in the Chesapeake Bay Watershed: A Regional Management Plan. Maryland Department of Natural Resources.

OTA (US Congress Office of Technology Assessment). 1993. Harmful Non-Indigenous Species in the United States. US Government Printing Office, Washington, DC.

Perles, S., J. Finley, and M. Marshall. 2009. Vegetation Monitoring Protocol for the Eastern Rivers and Mountains Network. Natural Resource Report NPS/ERMN/NRR—2009/DRAFT. National Park Service. Fort Collins, CO.

Rejmánek, M., and M. J. Pitcairn. 2002. When is eradication of exotic plant pests a realistic goal?. Pages. 169–176. *in* Veitch CR, Clout MN, eds. Turning the Tide: The Eradication of Invasive Species. Gland (Switzerland): IUCN.

Rozenfelds, A. C. F., L. Cave, D. I. Morris, and A. M. Buchanan. 1999. The weed invasion in Tasmania since 1970. Australian Journal of Botany 47:23–48.

Spaulding, S., and L. Elwell. 2007. Increase in nuisance blooms and geographic expansion of the freshwater diatom Didymosphenia geminate: Recommendations for response. White paper. 33 pp. [http://www.macfff.org/pdf/ScientificKnowledgeofDidymo.pdf]. Accessed December 1, 2009.

Timmins, S. M., and H. Braithwaite. 2001. Early detection of invasive weeds on islands. Pages 311–318 *In* Veitch, C. R., and M. N. Clout (eds.). Turning the tide: the eradication of invasive species. IUCN SSC Invasive Specialist Group. IUCN, Gland, Switzerland and Cambridge, UK.

U.S. Presidential Executive Order (USPEO). 1999. Executive Order 13112 of February 3, 1999. Federal Register: February 8, 1999 (Volume 64, Number 25).

Williams, A. E., S. O'Neil, E. Speith, and J. Rodgers. 2007. Early Detection Monitoring of Invasive Plant Species in the San Francisco Bay Area Network: A Volunteer-Based Approach. Natural Resource Report NPS/PWR/SFAN/NRR—2007/00N. National Park Service Pacific West Regional Office, Oakland, CA.

Table A1. Summary score card of early detection plant and pest species for Bluestone National Scenic River (BLUE).

Scientific Name	Common Name	Year Detected		Action			
		2008	2009	Treated or Removed	No Action	Treatment Planned	Reported to EDDMapS[*]
PEST							
Agrilus planipennis	emerald ash borer						
HERB							
Dioscorea oppositifolia	Chinese yam						
Heracleum mantegazzium	giant hogweed						
Phragmites australis	phragmites						
Polygonum cuspidatum/P. sachalinense	Japanese/giant knotweed	X[#]		X			X
Ranunculus ficaria	lesser celandine						
Oplismenus hirtellus ssp. *undulatifolius*	wavyleaf basketgrass						
VINE							
Celastrus orbiculata	Oriental bittersweet						
Polygonum perfoliatum	mile-a-minute						
Pueraria montana var. *lobata*	kudzu						
SHRUB							
Berberis thunbergii	Japanese barberry						
Frangula alnus	glossy buckthorn						
Rhamnus cathartica	common buckthorn						
TREE							
Acer platanoides	Norway maple						

[*] As of January 2010, only plant observations can be entered into EDDMapS. As the Mid Atlantic Mapping System is developed as part of EDDMapS, the ability to enter and view maps of pest detections will be added in the future.

[#] Species originally discovered in 11/28/2003 by contractor, but was re-visited and treated in 2009 as a result of the development and initiation of the ISED protocol.

Table A2. Summary score card of early detection plant and pest species for Delaware Water Gap National Recreation Area (DEWA).

Scientific Name	Common Name	Year Detected		Action			
		2008	2009	Treated or Removed	No Action	Treatment Planned	Reported to EDDMapS[*]
PEST							
Agrilus planipennis	emerald ash borer						
Anoplophora glabripennis	Asian longhorned beetle						
Pyrrhalta viburni	viburnum leaf beetle		X[#]		X		
Sirex noctillio	sirex woodwasp						
HERB							
Cardamine impatiens	narrowleaf bittercress	X	X	X		X	X
Heracleum mantegazzium	giant hogweed						
Phragmites australis	phragmites						
Ranunculus ficaria	lesser celandine						
Oplismenus hirtellus ssp. *undulatifolius*	wavyleaf basketgrass						
VINE							
Cynanchum spp.	swallowworts						
Polygonum perfoliatum	mile-a-minute						
Pueraria montana var. *lobata*	kudzu						
SHRUB							
Aralia elata	Japanese aralia						
Frangula alnus	glossy buckthorn						
Viburnum dilatatum	linden arrowwood		X	X			X
TREE							
Phellodendron amurense	Amur corktree		X	X			X

[*] As of January 2010, only plant observations can be entered into EDDMapS. As the Mid Atlantic Mapping System is developed as part of EDDMapS, the ability to enter and view maps of pest detections will be added in the future.
[#] Evidence was reported to the Department of Agriculture and species confirmation is needed before the detection can be listed in the National Agricultural Pest Information System (NAPIS).

Table A3. Summary score card of early detection plant and pest species for Friendship Hill National Historic Site (FRHI).

Scientific Name	Common Name	Year Detected		Action			
		2008	2009	Treated or Removed	No Action	Treatment Planned	Reported to EDDMapS[*]
PEST							
Agrilus planipennis	emerald ash borer						
Anoplophora glabripennis	Asian longhorned beetle						
Pyrrhalta viburni	viburnum leaf beetle						
Sirex noctillio	sirex woodwasp						
HERB							
Cardamine impatiens	narrowleaf bittercress						
Heracleum mantegazzium	giant hogweed						
Phragmites australis	phragmites						
Ranunculus ficaria	lesser celandine						
Oplismenus hirtellus ssp. undulatifolius	wavyleaf basketgrass						
VINE							
Polygonum perfoliatum	mile-a-minute						
Pueraria montana var. lobata	kudzu						
SHRUB							
Euonymus alatus	winged burning bush						
Ligustrum spp.	privet	X			X		X
Rhamnus cathartica	common buckthorn						

As of January 2010, only plant observations can be entered into EDDMapS. As the Mid Atlantic Mapping System is developed as part of EDDMapS, the ability to enter and view maps of pest detections will be added in the future.

Table A4. Summary score card of early detection plant and pest species for Gauley River National Recreation Area (GARI).

Scientific Name	Common Name	Year Detected		Action			
		2008	2009	Treated or Removed	No Action	Treatment Planned	Reported to EDDMapS*
PEST							
Agrilus planipennis	emerald ash borer						
HERB							
Alliaria petiolata	garlic mustard						
Dioscorea oppositifolia	Chinese yam						
Heracleum mantegazzium	giant hogweed						
Lespedeza cuneata	Chinese lespedeza						
Lythrum salicaria	purple loosestrife						
Phragmites australis	phragmites						
Polygonum cuspidatum/P. sachalinense	Japanese/giant knotweed	X				X	X
Ranunculus ficaria	lesser celandine						
Oplismenus hirtellus ssp. undulatifolius	wavyleaf basketgrass						
VINE							
Celastrus orbiculata	Oriental bittersweet						
Polygonum perfoliatum	mile-a-minute						
Pueraria montana var. lobata	kudzu						
SHRUB							
Berberis thunbergii	Japanese barberry						
Frangula alnus	glossy buckthorn						
Rhamnus cathartica	common buckthorn						
TREE							
Acer platanoides	Norway maple						

As of January 2010, only plant observations can be entered into EDDMapS. As the Mid Atlantic Mapping System is developed as part of EDDMapS, the ability to enter and view maps of pest detections will be added in the future.

Table A5. Summary score card of early detection plant and pest species for New River Gorge National River (NERI).

Scientific Name	Common Name	Year Detected		Action			
		2008	2009	Treated or Removed	No Action	Treatment Planned	Reported to EDDMapS[*]
PEST							
Agrilus planipennis	emerald ash borer		X[#]			X	
Lymantria dispar	gypsy moth		X		X		
HERB							
Heracleum mantegazzium	giant hogweed						
Ranunculus ficaria	lesser celandine						
Oplismenus hirtellus ssp. *undulatifolius*	wavyleaf basketgrass						
VINE							
Polygonum perfoliatum	mile-a-minute						
SHRUB							
Berberis thunbergii	Japanese barberry		X	X			X
Frangula alnus	glossy buckthorn						
Rhamnus cathartica	common buckthorn						
TREE							
Acer platanoides	Norway maple						

* As of January 2010, only plant observations can be entered into EDDMapS. As the Mid Atlantic Mapping System is developed as part of EDDMapS, the ability to enter and view maps of pest detections will be added in the future.
# Emerald ash borer presence discovered and confirmed by the Animal and Plant Health Inspection Service (APHIS).

NPS 962/101470, March 2010

www.ingramcontent.com/pod-product-compliance
Lightning Source LLC
Chambersburg PA
CBHW080936290526
45795CB00007BA/2781